COMPOSER SHOWCASE
HAL LEONARD STUDENT PIANO LIBRARY

Dances from Around the World

SEVEN SOLOS IN NATIONAL STYLES

BY CHRIST⸰ ⸰SAROS

T0210302

Acknowledgement:
I would like to extend special thanks to Margaret Otwell
for her excellent advice and careful attention to detail.

CONTENTS

Editor: Margaret Otwell

ISBN-13: 978-1-4234-2209-9
ISBN-10: 1-4234-2209-0

HAL•LEONARD®
CORPORATION
7777 W. BLUEMOUND RD. P.O. BOX 13819 MILWAUKEE, WI 53213

In Australia Contact:
Hal Leonard Australia Pty. Ltd.
4 Lentara Court
Cheltenham, Victoria, 3192 Australia
Email: ausadmin@halleonard.com

Visit Hal Leonard Online at
www.halleonard.com

Performance Notes

"Siciliana" was conceived in the *cantabile* Italian style found in such pieces as the second movement of Mozart's *Concerto No. 23 in A Major, KV 488*, and Fauré's own *Sicilienne*. An expressive phrasing, lightly emphasizing the non-harmonic tones, will enable the performer to bring out the soulfulness of this piece. The middle section (mm. 17-33) has an enigmatic quality through the use of the melodic-minor mode. In mm. 50 to the end, allow the sound to dissipate in a faint sound color.

"Menuet Pastoral" is to be performed with elegance and a light bounce. A carefully balanced sound, particularly as the melody shifts between the two hands, is essential to create a sort of dialogue between different instruments. It may be helpful to imagine the sound of a flute in the first four measures and that of a cello in the tenor part of mm. 5-6.

"Norwegian Dance," inspired by folk tales of sprites and dwarfs, is intended to sound mysterious and feathery. To this end, strive for very soft, yet crisp left-hand eighth notes. The piece starts with a distant, almost indefinite sound that becomes more present with the beginning of each phrase (mm. 5, 16, 27 and 35). The *molto meno mosso* section in mm. 57-63 portrays noble bowing gestures, while in the ensuing *tempo primo* ending phrase one can picture a group of odd little dancing creatures suddenly disappearing in a whiff.

"Little Mazurka" stems from my personal experiences in Poland while I was a student. This particular dance is in the moderate *mazur* type, as opposed to the slower and serious *kujawiak* and the faster, circle-type *oberek*. In the F major section, the left hand features the drone effect of the *dudy*, an instrument similar to the bagpipe often used to accompany mazurkas in old times. To simulate this effect, keep the left hand softer throughout this section and use the *una corda* pedal on the repeat.

"Gypsy Dance" evokes a joyful, outdoor fair with gypsy violins and lively dancers swirling in circles and rows. Every phrase can be imagined in terms of different dance formations. Using this imagery as a tool can help to bring this colorful music to life. The left-hand articulation is essential to bring out the energetic character of the dance.

Inspired by Tchaikovsky's lyrical style, "Waltz" features a lighthearted, subtle melody evoking a graceful skate dance in a French romantic flavor. Keep the beginning of the B-flat major section in a true piano dynamic, very subtly bringing out the left hand; later, be certain to make a beautiful *crescendo* in mm. 41-43, creating a dynamic arch, much in the way of the sun rising over a snowy landscape.

"Cossack Dance" is a collage of the many facets of a lively celebration: the arrival of the musicians (mm. 9), the gathering of the dancers (mm. 10-16), the stomping and jumping of proud Cossacks (mm. 18-40), and accordions with other folk instruments (mm. 43-49). The dance builds progressively to a frenzy and, much in the Russian tradition, it suddenly comes to a halt (mm. 40 and 68) to resume with renewed energy after the long-held *fermata*. The *pesante* section (mm. 52-58) can be imagined in terms of the generous leaping and squatting gestures of the male dancers while the following *leggiero* section (mm. 60-67) illustrates the opposing female section in light, hopping steps.

In memory of Andrew

Siciliana

Christos Tsitsaros

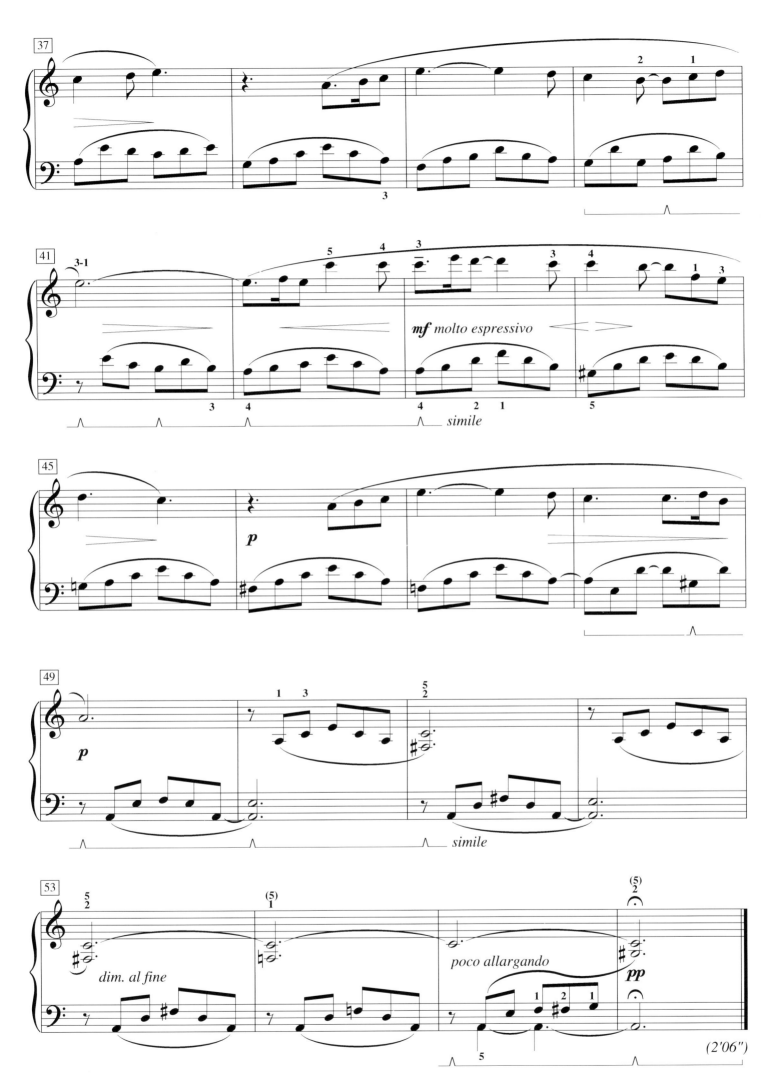

To Margaret Otwell

Menuet Pastoral

Christos Tsitsaros

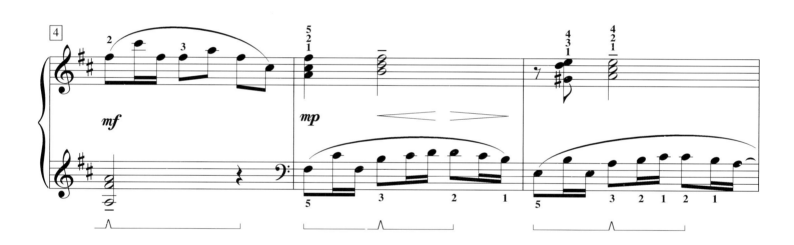

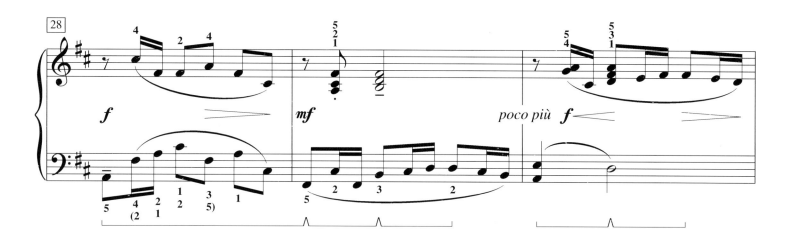

(1'12")

To Kim Chinquee

Norwegian Dance

Christos Tsitsaros

10

calando e rit.

Molto meno mosso (♩ = 58)

mp

espressivo e cantabile

tre corde

R.H. over

Tempo primo (♩ = 144)

pp a tempo

u.c.

leggierissimo

8va

(1'07")

11

To James Lyke

Little Mazurka

Christos Tsitsaros

poco rit.

mp
a tempo

mf
1/5 (second time una corda)
2/5
2/5

2nd time D.C. al Fine

(second time play pp)

1'17"

To Marika Iyer

Gypsy Dance

Christos Tsitsaros

15

To Ludmila Ivanovna

Waltz
(Valse de Patinage)

Christos Tsitsaros

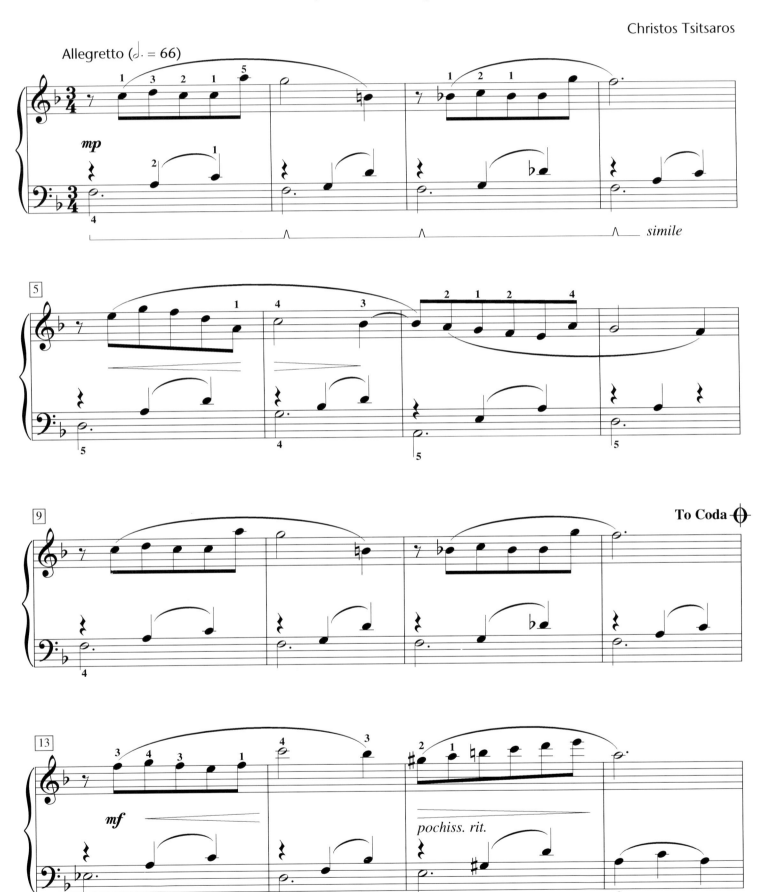

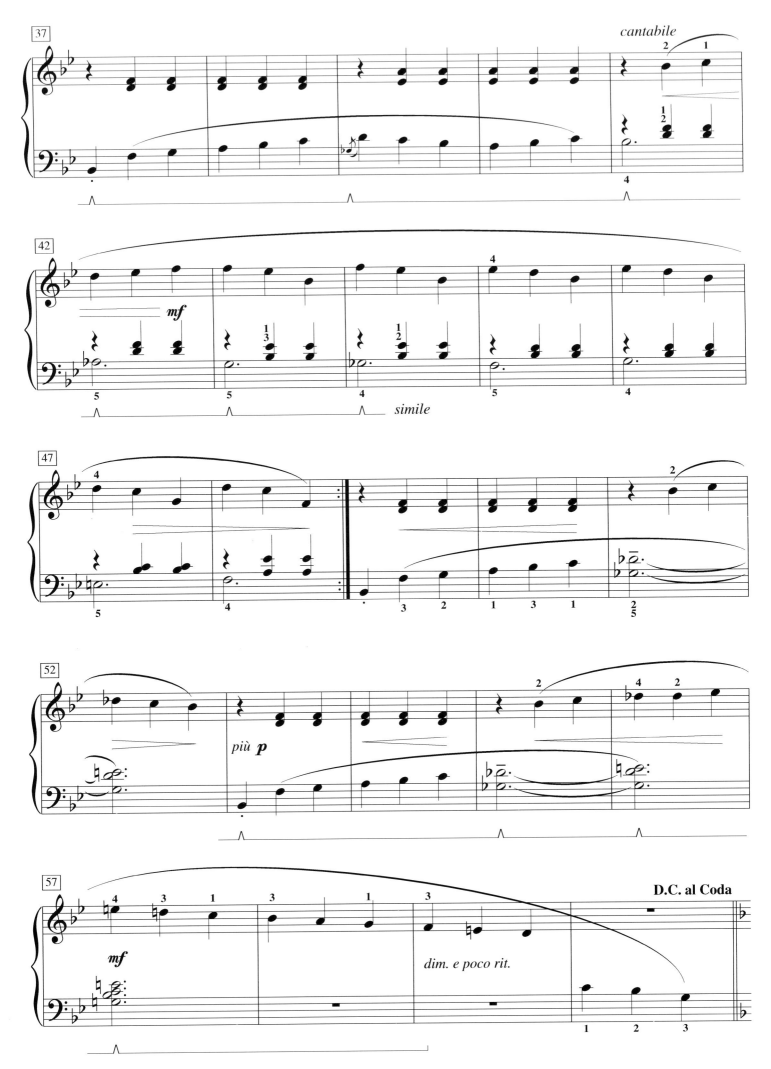

(1'24")

To Jouri Maevski

Cossack Dance

Christos Tsitsaros

(senza pedale)

molto cresc. e | poco accelerando

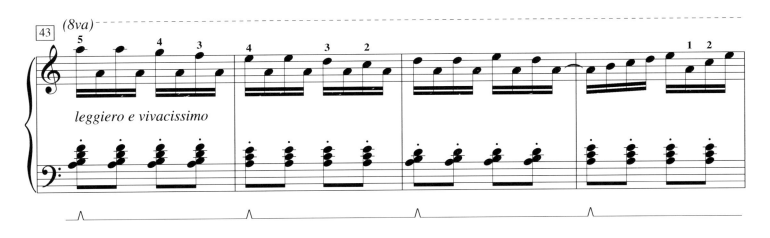

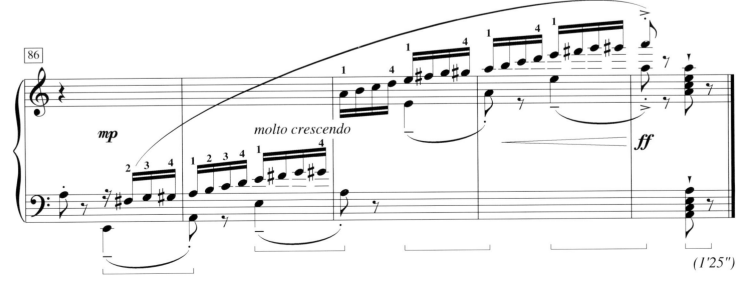